SEE SPOT RUN

SEE

SPOT

RUN

BACK-TO-BASICS
MANAGEMENT
"THAT WORKS"

KEVIN J. MURPHY

<u>ELI</u>

ISBN: 1-879501-01-5
Library of Congress Catalog Card #

ELI Press
(Effective Listening® Institute)
P.O. Box 1523
198 Main Street
Salem, NH 03079
(603) 898-9372

Printed in the United States of America
10 9 8 7 6 5 4 3 2 1   94 93 92 91 90

To my wife, Dolores, and my children Kevin,
Christina, and Kerri, for their patience and understanding
during the preparation of this book.

Also, to all my valued clients who have believed in
and trusted my common-sense approaches to addressing
business problems.

Contents

PART II. Practical Approaches to Hiring, Managing, and Motivating Good Employees

PART III. Responsive Actions That Show Customers You Care About Their Business

Introduction

Remember your first book? It was so simplistic. The sentences were short and concise. Ideas were understandable. The approach was solid and basic. It was the best way to learn a complex skill. But, a lot has happened since we first SAW SPOT RUN.

We have endured years of education, experienced a variety of jobs, and faced a multitude of complicated situations. Along the way we have accumulated a great deal of information, facts and ideas . . . some very useful . . . others not.

And, with the proliferation of technology, there's no end to the details, figures and statistics that flood our minds. This is especially true when it comes to directing a business.

In an effort to stay in touch with leading-edge management trends, we have drifted away from basic, common-sense approaches that really work.

Contrary to popular belief, it isn't necessary to be a rocket scientist to run a business, successfully manage people, or implement creative sales programs. All it takes is basic common sense to arrive at practical solutions to business-related issues. But today we seem to have a knack for complicating our lives by circumventing problems, challenges, and opportunities. We continue, in the spirit of the Information Age, to study and analyze issues to death.

Because of phenomenal growth and profits, this quantitative approach to business was condoned and allowed to flourish during the 1980s. Middle managers enjoyed the financial luxury of dancing around the issues and creating hierarchies to support many nonproductive activities. However, at the end of the decade, international economic pressures coupled with consolidations exposed the inefficiencies of this layer of management. The result . . . the elimination of over 3 million middle management positions.

The reduction of middle management jobs was no accident. As a byproduct of this shakeout, many corporations discovered that they operated with a better feel for their business when fewer reporting layers existed between the top executives and the customers. Their discovery was the beginning of a trend in which top executives have more contact and influence over daily business activities.

Today, in an oversupplied world, executives, employees, customers, and suppliers must all work closely together to survive difficult economic times. To meet this challenge, executives, managers, and salespeople will have to call upon common-sense *Management That Works* to arrive at practical solutions to rising costs, competitive pressures, and personnel-related problems.

Management That Works reveals thirty basic approaches to dealing with the most common problems and misconceptions, which I have repeatedly uncovered in speeches and consultations with thousands of executives over the past ten years. This book provides an easy-to-read reference that will help reduce complicated issues into fundamental and consistent solutions in three key areas.

1. *Policymaking.* The first part of this book covers important issues for constructing a corporation with a solid foundation built upon basic policies and philosophies. Job satisfaction is thoroughly discussed, with emphasis on instilling company pride and team spirit. Issues critical to the bottom line, such as collect-

ing receivables, utilizing strategic plans, and developing a positive corporate culture are all addressed in detail.

    2. *Managing.* The second section provides practical steps for selecting, managing, and motivating employees. Discover the difference between a sapper and a zapper. Find out how to curtail layoffs. Know what type of training new managers need to survive. This section also focuses on selecting the right people for key positions, challenging these people, and translating their success into realistic expectations.

    3. *Selling and servicing the customer.* The final chapters of this book deal with selling and servicing customers. Learn why three words, "Is that it," cost companies millions each year. Discover how customer complaints can open new doors and enhance company stature. Learn how to recognize the qualities that keep customers coming back. Find out how to effectively manage telecommunication automation. This section also explains the difference between *cost* and *price* and its effect on the bottom line.

    An objective for all busy executives should be to read one chapter a day for the next 30 days. It won't take that much time and effort, but it will be a chance to investigate some critical issues.

    Management That Works will not replace a four-year degree at an accredited university, but it is an effective starting point on the way to earning your Ph.D. in basic common-sense management.

To build company pride, you need a stable work environment and a strong sense of purpose.

PART I

Policies and Philosophies That Create a Proud and Successful Team

We learn by observing
the actions of people we
admire and respect.

CHAPTER 1

Company Pride Starts at the Top

Company pride is contagious. It builds enthusiasm and creates a sense of purpose for all employees. When employees feel good about their company, everybody, including their customers, knows it.

Pride starts with the company's top executives. It is a direct reflection of their attitudes, ethics, and approach to dealing with customers and employees. If the owner of a small gas station believes washing windshields is important, so will the attendants. If a manager in a factory takes pride in handling the small details affecting his subordinates, they will also pay attention to detail.

More than ever before, consumers are placing a higher value on service when making purchasing decisions. Service is a direct reflection of how a company feels about itself and its customers.

How often do you measure the capabilities of a doctor by the receptionist's attitude, the attire of the waiting room, and the condition of the magazines? Why did you drive past the gas station that looked greasy and old even though you were in a hurry?

— ❖ —

COMPANY PRIDE ENHANCES EMPLOYEE
SELF-ESTEEM.

— ❖ —

Company pride is not just talk. It is action. A flight attendant who works for the airline that "Loves to fly and it shows" relayed a story about a baggage handler who dropped a passenger's luggage while loading it onto the plane. As the passenger watched from the first-class cabin, the suitcase flew open and clothes scattered all over the ground. The passenger went to the galley and started screaming at the baggage handler through the open door. Several minutes later the baggage handler boarded the plane, sought out the passenger whose luggage had been dropped, and apologized for the miscue. The flight attendant's reaction: "I was never so proud to work for this airline." The passenger's comment to another traveler: "This airline is the best; they really care and take pride in their work."

People want to be associated with winners. It is natural, and it benefits a person's self-esteem. Customers will pay higher prices to conduct business with class acts. And these customers will be more than happy to tell others about the first-rate suppliers they deal with. Employees will accept lower wages to be part of a winning team that has a good name and reputation. Success boosts employee morale, which creates a great working environment. When this happens, the job often becomes primary and the wages secondary.

Want to gauge company pride? The next time you meet a new acquaintance, ask what he or she does for a living. Those with a strong sense of pride will tell you their company before their job function. However, when you hear "I'm a salesman for a consumer products company" you know the pride is missing.

To build this pride in any company or organization, both the physical plant and the mental environment must be addressed. Generating pride can be as easy and as fundamental as cleaning the washrooms more frequently, painting the walls in the plant, providing proper lighting and climate control, or supplying new uniforms with the company logo.

—— ❖ ——

SUCCESSFUL BUSINESSES ARE PERCEIVED AS
HAVING AN EXTREMELY HIGH LEVEL
OF PRIDE.

—— ❖ ——

PRIDE COMES TO THOSE WHO REALLY CARE.

—— ❖ ——

Pride can also be instilled by welcoming back employees from vacation, contacting sick employees to see how they are feeling, taking interest in all facets of employees' job descriptions, talking to employees about company problems, sharing managerial ideas, or even something as simple as saying "hello" or "good morning." These few pride generators can make the difference between a staff brimming with company pride or a staff filled with company distaste.

Be patient. Developing lasting pride takes time, nurturing, and a history of consistent actions that demonstrate attitudes, ethics, and approaches that employees and customers can be proud of.

When employees enjoy
their work it shows.

CHAPTER 2

Having Fun—The Key
to Team Spirit

Everything I needed to know about teamwork I learned from my daughter's softball coaches.

Watching the Blue Jays practice on a cold April afternoon, I could not help wondering how these awkward and inexperienced little girls could ever win a single game. Ground balls trickled through their legs, popped flies landed everywhere but in their gloves, and pitches were missed time and time again. The poor coaches!

But something started to happen to this group of young women.

"Daddy, practice was great today. *We* learned to run . . . *We* learned to slide . . . *We* learned to bunt . . . *We* even have signals that only our *team* knows. Daddy, I love softball; it's so much fun, and my teammates are all great kids."

These eager, impressionable kids were being taught how to play as a team by very skillful, warm, and caring coaches. Basics were stressed, having fun was a priority, and winning was only to be a byproduct of both. There were no superstars, no individual awards. Everyone played each game, players

— ❖ —

COACHES' FORMULA FOR WINNING:

BE CONSTRUCTIVE
CARE
STRESS THE POSITIVE
KEEP TO THE BASICS
SHOW RESPECT
HAVE FUN

— ❖ —

were not pulled when they made errors, and marginal calls by the umpires were accepted without disagreement.

The coaches never criticized any player. They continually stressed the positive aspects of the girls' performance, held pep talks between innings, and instilled confidence in the little girls.

Along with the coaches' assistance, parental support and participation was high. Kids traveled from vacations to make the play-offs, and absenteeism at games and practices was almost nonexistent. This group of inexperienced little girls became a "team." They worked hard, respected their leaders, recognized their dependence on each other, learned the effectiveness of team work and, most importantly, had fun in the process.

Managers, take note, because the following ingredients build a successful team spirit.

- *Be a constructive rather than a destructive coach.* Tell employees what has to be done. They will figure out the best way to do it. Assist in setting goals and objectives for everybody. They will then know what is expected and will appreciate it. Use constructive criticism only as a vehicle for improvement and never as a tool for gaining power.

- *Show that you care about the players on your team.* Talk with your employees, not at them. Listen . . . listen . . . listen. It may surprise you to find that they know some of the answers you are looking for.

- *Always stress the positive.* Negativism can only damage the delicate manager–employee relationship. Everybody, no matter how inconsequential, has positive energy that can be channeled effectively. Build on the positive.

——— ❖ ———

SOPHISTICATION CAN BE TOO
SOPHISTICATED—
STICK TO THE BASICS.

——— ❖ ———

WINNING ISN'T EVERYTHING UNLESS IT
IS FUN.

——— ❖ ———

- *Never forget the basics.* Don't try to be too sophisti-cated. It may look and sound good but will only wind up causing confusion. Work on the fundamental skills that will allow the employees to win.

- *Show respect and honor for each team member.* Even though you are managing a company or an office, you are managing individuals. All employees can make contributions. When they do, show some respect and honor. Don't be afraid to say, "We are fortunate to have you on our team."

- *Have fun.* The manager who can make the work fun will be blessed with a spirit that is conducive to winning. However, winning isn't everything unless it is fun. When the employees enjoy themselves and experience success, they will perceive work as fun.

Being the type of manager who embodies these qualities can transform a lackluster, disorganized organization into a "team."

Just in case you wished to know, the little Blue Jays finished first and won every game in the play-offs. Not bad for a "team" having fun.

Spending too much
time in too many meetings
can result in one final
meeting.

CHAPTER 3

Meetings Require Structure and Objectives

"Bob, we must schedule another meeting to discuss if the meeting we just finished covered all the major points of yesterday's meeting." Does this sound all too familiar?

If you are concerned about ineffective meetings, ask yourself the following questions:

Do you spend more than thirty percent of your time in meetings?

Do meetings commonly take precedence over addressing customer problems?

Is your first reaction to a problem to call a meeting?

Do your spouse, friends, or colleagues ever comment that it seems like all you ever do is go to meetings?

If you answered "yes" to any of these questions, you could be a candidate for the Meetings Hall of Fame.

MEETINGS ARE EXPENSIVE!

The most significant common thread found in financially troubled companies is too many insignificant and unstructured meetings. In fact, a survey conducted by our consulting firm revealed that top-level managers spend nearly sixty percent of their time in meetings.

Make no mistake about it: *meetings are expensive.*

Unfortunately, most companies do not think of meetings in terms of their relative cost. For example, a weekly meeting of five executives who earn an average of $80,000 per year costs a company over $27,000. This translates to a minimum of $150,000 in incremental sales just to cover the cost of the meeting.

Besides their cost, meetings can be used as a crutch by employees who are not working to capacity. And if a company employs a group of people without full plates of work, the hunger for more unnecessary meetings will increase.

Because of these drawbacks, it is easy to understand why the business meeting gets so much negative publicity. Most managers and employees look at meetings as wastes of time, gripe sessions, or ego builders for upper-level management.

Now for the good news about meetings. They can be an effective vehicle for several management goals.

- *Solving problems:* "How can we instill company pride after laying off twenty percent of the workforce?" *or* "Why are sales off by twenty percent versus the same period last year?"

- *Instilling team spirit:* "Everybody in this company has to pull together through these lean economic times." *or* "The major reason people work is to make money. There's no way that can happen in this company unless we start acting like a team."

— ❖ —

MEETINGS SHOULD NOT BE CRUTCHES FOR
MENTALLY INCAPACITATED MANAGERS.

— ❖ —

KEYS TO SUCCESSFUL MEETINGS:

SET OBJECTIVES
LIMIT PARTICIPATION TO CONTRIBUTORS
EXPRESS THE NEED
STRESS PREPARATION
ESTABLISH A TIME LIMIT

— ❖ —

- *Recognizing contributions:* "The research and development department has successfully cut costs by fifteen percent while production was up ten percent." *or* "All the research you did over the past month did pay off. Our forecast for the third quarter was right on the money."

- *Making introductions:* "We have three new and experienced people joining our winning sales staff." *or* "These are the products we will introduce at this year's trade show."

- *Developing innovations:* "All the departments have to join in the effort to come up with alternatives for waste disposal." *or* "We need suggestions on how to automate our office systems."

- *Conceptualizing plans and objectives:* "Since the recent change in the demographics, we have to shift our attention to the new kind of customers we want to attract. What is the company's mission now?" *or* "Based on our increased customer base, we have to set new goals for production."

- *Implementing change:* "The recent change in relations with the labor union has implications for our marketing methods. What are the implications, and how do they affect our approach?" *or* "What can be done to meet the production quota?"

With those ideas in mind, ask yourself the following questions before you plan your next meeting:

Does the meeting have specific objectives?

Have I limited participation to those who will contribute?

Is everyone aware of the need for the meeting?

Is everyone prepared for the meeting?

Have I set a time limit for the meeting?

Answer "no" to any of the above and you will be setting yourself up for a costly forum that could result in misunderstanding, finger pointing, and dispersion of accountability. However, if you develop a reputation for holding meetings that are worthwhile, well-run, and completed on time, they can be one of your most effective management tools.

Time to go now. It seems I have been asked to attend a very important meeting to analyze why we have so many meetings.

CHAPTER 4

Strategic Plans Are Necessary for Survival

Short-term success can be fleeting. It can lure businesspeople into thinking growth will continue indefinitely without any planning or actions to prepare for the future.

For example, one of our clients received a rather unexpected multimillion-dollar order from a new customer to manufacture several highly machined parts. This new order, which had a six-month release cycle, disrupted the factory. The employees were pushed to meet the demands of the new deal while trying to keep up with their regular production.

A tremendous strain was also placed on this manufacturer's suppliers. Purchasing agents had to place sizable orders with suppliers who weren't expecting them. Inventories, as well as solid working relationships, were pushed to the limit on both sides. Ultimately, the disruption resulted in late shipments to current customers. These customers noticed a change and started to move longstanding business to my client's competition.

— ❖ —

SHORT-TERM SUCCESS DOESN'T FORE-SHADOW LONG-TERM GROWTH.

— ❖ —

Everyone was jumping through hoops to impress this *one* new customer, whose business was not forecast or mentioned in any sales plans.

Suddenly, after six months, orders stopped flowing from the new account. Our client discovered that the new customer's former supplier had just been awarded a multiyear contract at higher prices. It appeared that the short-term orders had been a ploy to solidify a strong position for upcoming negotiations with the former supplier.

This short-lived boon then became the proverbial baboon on the company's back, which was already aching after jumping through all those hoops. The loss of this business negatively affected costs, raised inventories, and damaged supplier confidence. Yet, all of this could have been avoided if a strategic plan had been in place.

With a good plan, questions like the following would have arisen:

- Why are we receiving unexpected business?

- Should we accept the order without a long-term commitment from the customer?

- What impact will this slug of business have on our costs and ability to service existing customers?

- Will our suppliers be able to fit into our plans?

- What will the impact be on the employees?

- Will we still be able to produce a good product?

- Will we have to hire more workers? How many? What departments?

— ❖ —

STRATEGIC PLANS MUST BE A COMPANY-
WIDE PROJECT.

— ❖ —

To develop technology and provide the products and services required by the market, strategic plans need the participation of the following functional groups.

Managers.   The first place to start the planning process is with department managers. They must have input, because they will be held accountable for the success of the plan. They must be confident that the plan is viable, because they must convince the workers.

Employees.   Also, employees should be permitted to participate in planning. Just like managers, they are key elements in a plan's success. If workers feel they are valued as contributors, they will do everything to see their contributions translate into successful results.

Suppliers.   Never overlook suppliers while developing a plan. Next to employees, suppliers know your business better than anyone. They may be able to add comments that will not only facilitate their planning but also enhance your business. This mutual relationship gives both parties the opportunity to take advantage of important research and forecasting information that is integral to any planning.

Customers.   Finally, look to your customers. They are the best indication of what the future holds. Ask any customer for opinions or evaluations and get ready to see the real world. Their visions have to be considered significant, because if any one group can alter the course of your business, it has to be your customers.

Consideration must also be given to the changing demographics in markets. A classic example has to be in the operation of a radio station. If the management doesn't pay any attention to audience statistics, it would be hard to figure out what kind of music or talk to air. However, if enough research is conducted, it should be simple for the station to play exactly what the audience wants, when they want it. If an understanding of the audience can be achieved, winning is only a matter of time. The same can be said of any business engaged in researching and planning.

—— ❖ ——

PLAN FOR YOUR COMPANY'S FUTURE BEFORE YOUR COMPETITION DOES.

—— ❖ ——

Likewise, it is necessary to keep track of the impact of consolidations and mergers on competitors and of the desire of your customers to purchase additional products from you.

Because technology changes rapidly, market structures are taking on different shapes through international mergers and acquisitions. Customers are becoming fewer, larger, and more sophisticated; they control tremendous purchasing power. To enhance customer relationships it is necessary to develop plans that insure delivering a product on time, at a competitive price, and with a commitment to service.

Growth and survival depend on the development of a strategic plan. If you don't have a plan, start now to develop one. Don't allow the market and your competitors to determine your destiny.

You are what you
appear to be to others.

CHAPTER 5

Create the Proper Perception Through Communication

"Is the glass half full or half empty?"

Consider your company's stature as the glass. What is your customers' and employees' perception of the glass?

Perception is reality. Yet, every day managers bask in the glow of what "should be," "could be," and "might be" while turning their heads from "what is." This conjured-up thinking, this laying aside of reality, is the major reason good employees fail and market shares slip.

After completing a customer survey for a major telecommunications company whose market prices were deteriorating, we uncovered a lack of confidence in this company—not from the customers, but from their own salesforce. Upon further investigation, it was discovered that management's actions of curtailing research and development expenditures,

—— ❖ ——

FORGET WHAT "SHOULD BE," "COULD BE,"
OR "MIGHT BE." INSTEAD, CONCENTRATE
ON "WHAT IS."

—— ❖ ——

AN ACCURATE PERCEPTION IS A TIE
TO REALITY.

—— ❖ ——

closing a nonproductive service center, and cutting two trade shows from the advertising budget were perceived negatively by the sales group.

Management felt they were taking responsible steps to protect employment and to insure a good bottom line. The salespeople interpreted the actions as lowering the value of their products and services, which translated into a lack of confidence in front of the customers.

Developing and maintaining a positive perception requires continuous communication and good listening skills. Managers must be willing to ask tough questions and be receptive to challenging responses. In the example, management could have avoided the problem by communicating the thinking behind their curtailments and by soliciting comments from the salesforce.

When communication stops, a huge void is created where fiction becomes reality, off-the-cuff comments are interpreted as facts, and absence is translated into a lack of caring.

Another example of misperception and miscommunication involved a textile company that had to eliminate six positions because of an unexpected drop in earnings. But two weeks before the layoffs, management had spent a significant amount of money on a new computer system. Not once did any of the managers explain the layoffs or the reasons for the expensive purchases. Consequently, the workers started to churn the rumor mill and morale reached an all-time low.

This negative energy could have been eased with appropriate communication. The employees wanted a chance to talk about possible solutions to the financial problems that might save jobs. They were ignored. Naturally, the employees' perception of the company executives was negative. This in turn affected the corporate culture, because the management failed to focus on the situation.

———— ❖ ————

IF CUSTOMERS OR EMPLOYEES TELL YOU THE
SERVICE STINKS, BELIEVE THEM. DIG UNTIL
YOU FIND OUT WHY AND ASK FOR HELP
IN SOLVING THE PROBLEMS.

———— ❖ ————

Therefore, to create an appropriate perception for employees and customers, managers *must* take two important steps.

- *Monitor reactions.* This is the first step toward insuring that the money spent on product promotion, advertising, service, training, and personnel development is securing the desired results. If workers or customers appear concerned, there is usually a good reason. Attention should be focused on "what is" not on "what should be."

- *Institute plans to insure program effectiveness.* Once negative reactions are investigated, the next step is to quickly modify practices and procedures based on employee and customer input. Ignoring this input will only promote an incorrect perception that in turn will create nonproductive activities, turnovers in the workforce, lost customers, and disgruntled employees.

If customers or employees tell you the service, products, or procedures stink, believe them. Dig until you find out why, and ask for help in solving the problems.

When concerns are voiced, *listen.* By being open-minded, you will be able to solicit the input necessary to match the perception of your company with reality.

You are only as good to
your customers as your
suppliers are to you.

CHAPTER 6

Suppliers Are Valuable Partners

The most overlooked and precious natural resource for a company has to be its suppliers. Apart from employees, no other single group has more information and knowledge about a company. Yet most businesses neglect to recognize the value of suppliers as critical partners. Your suppliers will often call on your customers in an effort to get their products approved for use in your operations.

If your suppliers maintain a presence with your customers, it is very important that they possess a positive perception of your company. Therefore, partnerships between companies and suppliers are critical. They can add to the positive corporate culture every company wants.

A case in point would be the prototype company–supplier relationship that developed in the U.S. auto industry after several years of deteriorating profits. It became clear to the "big three" auto makers that their suppliers had both the resources and personnel necessary to reduce research and development expenditures by working as a team on new models.

— ❖ —

YOUR SUPPLIERS KNOW YOUR COMPANY
BETTER THAN YOU THINK.

— ❖ —

ESTABLISHING A PARTNERSHIP WITH
YOUR SUPPLIERS IS THE KEY TO BUILDING
MARKET SOLIDARITY.

— ❖ —

This move so significantly affected profits that auto manu-facturers established internal departments whose only func-tion was, and still is, to maintain good supplier relations.

Companies can develop good relations with suppliers by instilling a philosophy whereby market, product, and compet-itive information is shared on a regular basis. This information can then be used to strengthen the company's and supplier's market solidity.

Purchasing managers must sell their suppliers on this partnership approach. Both parties will then be better equipped to:

Develop technology.

Train personnel.

Generate leads.

This policy will insure mutual growth, development, and pros-perity.

But true partnerships with suppliers don't just happen. They are cultivated over a long period by demonstrating respect for the supplier's personnel and by recognizing the supplier's need to generate a reasonable profit.

In short, make every reasonable effort to keep suppliers happy and healthy, as they are the lifeblood of any company.

Try following the guidelines below to foster a better rela-tionship with suppliers.

- Don't keep salespeople waiting long in the reception area.

- Establish reasonable lead times for purchases.

- Avoid taking cash discounts after the appropriate time.

—— ❖ ——

TREATING SUPPLIERS LIKE CUSTOMERS INSURES YOUR SUCCESS.

—— ❖ ——

- Attempt to pay invoices on time. If you are having trouble paying the bills, tell the suppliers up front, and they will surely work with you.

- Ask suppliers to rate your performance as a customer. Their answers may be quite surprising. But once constructive advice is offered, act on it.

- Treat your suppliers like customers. This is the bottom line.

Once these guidelines are utilized to establish a working relationship with suppliers, business-related dilemmas can be handled through an effective partnership.

Taking on marginal accounts can cause a marginal performance with your existing customers.

CHAPTER 7

Too Many Customers Can Hurt Profits

WARNING: Having too many customers can be hazardous to your company's health.

This statement was brought to light by one of our clients that produces plastic parts for heavy industry. The customer base had increased from 400 to 1,200 accounts over a three-year period, but with only a ten percent growth in sales and no increase in profits.

Upon investigation, it was discovered that most of the accounts were small buyers that added significantly to the company's finished goods inventory and took up a disproportionate amount of the sales department's time.

By establishing a minimum order, assigning small accounts to distributors, and eliminating obsolete inventory, this company reduced its customer base by 1,000 accounts and enjoyed a twenty-five percent increase in both profits and sales during the next two years. Salespeople stopped hearing negative comments about assistance and attention. The customers were happy.

——— ❖ ———

BE A SIGNIFICANT SUPPLIER TO YOUR
CUSTOMERS AND A SIGNIFICANT CUSTOMER
TO YOUR SUPPLIERS.

——— ❖ ———

PLAYING HARD BALL WITH SUPPLIERS TO
CONTROL COSTS IS NO LONGER A HIT.

——— ❖ ———

The logical strategy for industrial companies in the 1990s is: *Be a significant supplier to your customers and a significant customer to your suppliers.* The days of protecting prices by playing hardball with multiple suppliers are gone. Confrontations are out. Partnerships are in. This process involves both the customer and supplier becoming mutually dependent on each other for success.

Reducing the supplier and customer base allows for significant growth at both ends of the business. This strategy will result in suppliers taking responsibility for just-in-time delivery of products, which will reduce inventory carrying costs. It is also possible to share in cost savings by providing annual commitments to the supplier. Ordering large quantities fewer times throughout the year can make for tremendous savings because of the discount possibilities. In turn, this approach also improves the production flow in the supplier's plant while enhancing the dependent relationship.

Being a key supplier will also help customers reduce their supplier base, which will in turn positively affect growth opportunities.

Another added benefit of this strategy is the capability to perform solid product forecasting. Because the customer and supplier are mutually dependent, an enormous amount of helpful information is available. Sharing these details could add significantly to correctly forecasting supply and demand figures. Accurate forecasting can reduce or increase production quotas, thus making it easier to control inventory costs.

All of this information can be summed up in two important points.

- *Limit suppliers and customers.* A limited number of suppliers coupled with a focused customer group will require fewer employees to provide customer service, manage inventories, and meet with suppliers. This limitation will increase profits, keep the customers at peace, and allow employees the time they need to do their jobs appropriately.

—— ❖ ——

DEVELOP CUSTOMERS—DON'T JUST
MAKE A SALE.

—— ❖ ——

- *Avoid short-term greediness.* The idea of adding customers for short-term gains doesn't necessarily insure profits. There will always be chances to make quick money with a significant sale.

With these points in mind, remember that complete attention should be placed on developing a solid customer base instead of just trying to make a sale.

Never be shy about asking for that which is rightfully yours.

CHAPTER 8

Overdue Receivables—Ask for the Money

"If it ain't broke, don't fix it!"

Isn't it truly amazing—yet unfortunate—how many managers use this expression each day, particularly when it comes to collecting receivables?

Certainly the adage has its roots in tradition, which has positive implications. Friendly's Ice Cream is a New England tradition. McDonald's is a tradition for fast food, worldwide. Coca Cola and Pepsi are traditional soft drinks. Toyota is a traditional import. All of these names owe their positive traditional images to offering a good product over a long period of time.

On the other hand, tradition may also hold negative implications. Just because something has survived time and is considered traditional, customary, or tolerable doesn't mean it "ain't broke."

A classic example of a business tradition that is "broke" and needs to be fixed is the way companies handle aging receivables. Unfortunately, unlike wine, receivables don't get

—— ❖ ——

UNLIKE WINE, RECEIVABLES DON'T GET
BETTER WITH AGE.

—— ❖ ——

better with age. When companies are quizzed about aging accounts, the most common responses are:

"If it ain't broke, don't fix it."

"It is customary and traditional for our industry to have receivables out so far."

"The customer is in good financial shape and will eventually pay."

"They are a good customer, and we don't want to insult them by asking for prompt payment."

Getting paid on time for goods and services is one of the most important factors in maintaining a healthy cash flow. But most businesses that extend credit find their average receivables running at a rate of ten to fifteen days beyond their standard terms of sale.

"Ask and you shall receive." Try applying this concept to receivables. Let customers know that payment is expected according to the terms and the condition of the sale.

In this case, it is beneficial to be conservative instead of liberal, tough instead of soft, or feared instead of loved. It is always better to be conservative, tough, or feared when it comes to receivables because once customers perceive you as liberal, soft, or loved, it will be difficult to change that perception when push comes to shove. A perception change will take considerable time and effort, and may possibly damage a company's stature. Lester G. Crocker says it best: "One can be feared without being hated."

Letting receivables ride beyond the payment period could have two damaging effects.

1. *Hurt cash flow and negatively affect prices.*   Not asking for money could send a signal to a shrewd buyer that margins are significant and carrying the receivable is built into the price. This is an asset to the buyer, but a liability to the seller.

—— ❖ ——

BEING LAX WITH RECEIVABLES SENDS
NEGATIVE MESSAGES ABOUT THE WAY
A COMPANY IS RUN.

—— ❖ ——

TRAIN YOUR CUSTOMERS TO PAY ON TIME.

—— ❖ ——

Also, many customers code their past payment experience and can tell you supplier by supplier how long they can withhold payment before the phone rings.

As a supplier you should be understanding of customers' business cycles, but not so lenient as to allow customers to start financing business with purchases from your company while hindering your cash flow.

2. *Damage company stature.*   Being lax with receivables can send a negative message to potential customers. Perception of a company is a direct reflection of its procedures and practices. Negligence with receivables may foreshadow shabbiness in production or inactivity in research and development.

If customers cannot pay within the terms of the sale, try the following procedures.

- Review and update customers' credit lines.

- Check with other suppliers selling to the same customers to confirm if they are having similar problems with the deficient accounts.

- Train your customers to pay on time. Modify their behavior by asking for prompt payment. It does work. Ask most accounts payable clerks who gets paid first and the response is almost unanimous: "The suppliers that bitch most frequently." If this is the case, why not try at least asking?

Remember, watching receivables is a clear indication that you need and expect payment. And more importantly, it is a signal that you are closely managing your business.

A favor done more
than once becomes an
obligation.

CHAPTER 9

Keep Company Benefits from Becoming Obligations

The company Christmas party. The traditional gift of a turkey at Thanksgiving. The personnel department's annual trip to the ball game.

Are these examples of great company benefits or corporate obligations? The answer rests in the minds of the beholders—your employees.

Events held more than once and repeated at the same time each year can lose their meaning as a benefit and quickly become a moral obligation, a tradition. But tradition can have a negative byproduct. Many employees feel that keeping with a tradition is an obligation of the employer. Any changes in the format or timing of the tradition can be interpreted as a lack of sensitivity toward the workers.

Consider one company that sponsored fifty-yard-line seats for all its employees at a football game. One year, because of the limited seating and an increase in employment, the company was only able to provide seats in the end zone. The employees' reaction was "The company is getting cheap."

— ❖ —

ANY CHANGE IN A COMPANY'S TRADITION
CAN BE INTERPRETED AS A LACK OF
SENSITIVITY TOWARD WORKERS.

— ❖ —

ANYTHING FREE HAS NO VALUE.

— ❖ —

KEEP BENEFITS A COMPANY OPTION.

— ❖ —

The idea of benefits being taken as obligations goes far beyond social events and gifts. It encompasses health plans, retirement programs, profit sharing, and social security. Any cost that is incurred for the employee by the company is a benefit. The challenge, then, is to educate each employee about the economic value of company-paid benefits.

The following guidelines have helped many companies highlight the out-of-pocket costs for benefit programs.

- *Share benefit–cost information.* Less than ten percent of the workforce knows that their employer has to match their social security payment. Break down the individual costs of all benefits paid for each employee and show them the dollar figure in writing each year. Many companies even print out the payments made by the insurance carrier for each employee.

  Other companies use the "cafeteria plan." Each employee is given a sum of money to be applied toward benefits. In this way it is easy for the workers to experience the ever-increasing costs of benefits.

- *Charge for social events.* The rule here is: anything free has no value. By charging even a token amount, the employees will realize that company-sponsored events are expensive. An employee who contributes fifteen dollars toward a guest's meal at a Christmas party will understand that the party has a minimum benefit of fifteen dollars.

- *Cancel events when business is off.* A company outing held two weeks after ten percent of the workforce has been laid off sends mixed signals. Employees should know when times are tough and should be called upon to make sacrifices. In fact, pulling together in hard times can make a stronger organization. Don't be embarrassed to cancel the Christmas party if the company is losing money.

By keeping benefits as a company's option, you can avoid creating many costly obligations in future years.

CHAPTER 10

Purchase on a Cost—
Not Price—Basis

Make no mistake about it, cost and price are two different things. Not realizing this can spell financial disaster.

Price is the dollar amount that appears on the invoice; cost is the real financial impact of employing a product in your operation. The concept of using *price* as the primary motivator for purchasing a product can result in additional costs that are buried in the product's use.

Take the example of a machinery manufacturer that purchases tool bits for drilling holes in heavy equipment. The price quotes received for the same size bit might vary by fifty percent. However, when employed in the actual operation, one bit may last three times longer, resulting in fewer rejects and enabling the operator to run the drill press at faster rates. The bottom line is: A half-price bit could actually cost more than twice as much to use.

Factors that need to be carefully examined in determining the true cost of an item are terms of sale, flexibility in the product's use, quality, impact of warranties, deliveries, shelf

—— ❖ ——

NOT KNOWING THE DIFFERENCE BETWEEN COST AND PRICE CAN SPELL FINANCIAL DISASTER.

—— ❖ ——

life, and any other factors affecting the efficiency of your operation.

The concept of purchasing based on value added versus price often breaks down because of corporate edicts and a lack of communication between the purchasing groups and the departments that use the product. This miscommunication can be costly, both monetarily and emotionally.

For instance, the manufacturing department of a high-tech plant needed to replace obsolescent machinery. The supervisor followed the chain of command and notified the president. The supervisor then met with the purchasing agents to report on what equipment was needed, based upon personal observations and past purchases. Purchasing then solicited bids. But not once were employees polled in an effort to nail down their suggestions or comments. The purchasing agents merely based their decisions on the lowest price and the suppliers' knowledge and opinions.

Based upon this scenario, the challenge for purchasing groups is to implement buying procedures without creating problems and destroying relationships.

To avoid disruptions, the purchasing department should gather clear specifications not only from qualified suppliers but also from department heads and their subordinates.

In addition, changing suppliers, even for the most insignificant products, can often have a subtle impact on the efficiency of other products employed in a manufacturing process. The best advice is to deal with suppliers who are reliable and dependable. Trying to save money by going with a new, untested supplier can be costly even though the price seems attractive. If there are significant delays in shipping or defects in the products, a tremendous amount of money and time could be lost to slow-downs and subassemblies.

—— ❖ ——

PURCHASING GROUPS NEED TO
COMMUNICATE WITH DEPARTMENTS TO
INSURE COST-EFFECTIVE PURCHASES

—— ❖ ——

That is precisely why suppliers who know the true value added of their quality products will be less inclined to cave in to price pressures. Suppliers who react quickly with price cuts are often marginal producers who either offer inferior products or lack understanding of their own costs.

The approach, then, is to think twice before buying on price, while encouraging your suppliers to demonstrate the true cost of buying their products. Don't take it personally when your suppliers' salespeople refuse to lower prices. In the long run they may be doing your company a great service.

We are most often
blind to the actions of
those closest to us.

CHAPTER 11

Monitor the Gatekeepers at the Executive Suite

The gatekeepers at executive suites can easily overstep their bounds and cause dissension, while their leaders feel all is well in the kingdom. We have all had experiences with interrogators, investigators, and martinets who feel it is their duty to insure that the chief is not disturbed with trivial matters—such as running a company.

Once I had dinner with a regional sales director of a local manufacturer who was thinking of leaving his company because he felt the CEO didn't respect his method of operation. When asked why he had this perception, he stated that none of his recent phone calls to the CEO on important sales matters had been returned. Knowing that this individual was a consistent performer, I approached the CEO the next day to gauge his feelings toward the manager. The chief expressed concern over this manager's lack of communication. "I have not talked with him in over a month." It turned out that the executive secretary had decided the calls were not urgent and so the messages had not been passed on to the top executive.

——— ❖ ———

IT SHOULDN'T BE A POLITICAL ISSUE TO SPEAK
WITH AN EXECUTIVE.

——— ❖ ———

This story is repeated daily, as top decision-makers develop blind spots to the performance of their assistants and their relative power within the company.

Three distinct problems always arise when executive assistants gain too much of a power base.

1. *Political posturing.* If executive secretaries don't like a particular manager, they can make it difficult for that individual to secure an audience with the CEO. Slowly but surely, employees and managers get the idea that only a chosen few can gain the privilege of talking to the boss. This will greatly affect the morale of the entire company because office politics will surface. Workers will then battle with each other to obtain the favor of the omnipotent gatekeeper in hopes of being awarded an appointment. This kind of political posturing causes havoc for the employees, but adds to the power base of the secretary.

2. *Loss of respect.* Another byproduct of an out-of-control assistant is loss of respect for the top executive. How often have you witnessed personnel policies on tardiness and sick days being violated most frequently by the office that is supposedly dictating the rules? With this type of atmosphere, the "Do as I say, not as I do" syndrome develops very quickly. This, of course, damages the reputation of the executive. It also creates a negative atmosphere that can destroy a positive corporate culture. Workers are willing to adhere to policies, but once they notice that certain people freely bypass or exempt themselves because of inherent power, the trouble starts. If the executive doesn't step in and rectify the situation, the employees will begin stirring the pot, which will diminish the executive's ability to lead. Policies are set to be followed—by everyone.

3. *Organizational detachment.* Corporate executives need to be accessible to feel the pulse of a company. By allowing an assistant to filter all calls, appointments, and correspondence, the CEO forfeits an opportunity to keep in touch with the organization. This detachment will be perceived negatively by workers and managers, who favor a hands-on approach by their leader. Another important factor is that many out-of-

——— ❖ ———

EXECUTIVES NEED TO BE ACCESSIBLE TO FEEL
THE PULSE OF THE COMPANY.

——— ❖ ———

EXECUTIVES SHOULD CAREFULLY MONITOR
THE POWER AN ASSISTANT MAY WIELD
WITHIN THE CORPORATE STRUCTURE.

——— ❖ ———

touch executives find, when they reconnect, that they have missed the daily involvement, which had helped them reach their status in the first place.

To avoid these three common problems, a most effective approach is to assign one assistant to a minimum of two executives. This action will insure an accurate perspective and quality-control check. It is then possible for the executives to meet and compare notes to make sure the assistant doesn't become too much of an insulating factor in the company.

As a top executive, step back and objectively review how your assistant projects your thoughts, concerns, and attitudes to the entire organization. You may discover that the executive suite houses two CEOs with totally different ideas on how the company should be run.

A manager is one of the
most important people in
an employee's life.

PART II

Practical Approaches to Hiring, Managing, and Motivating Good Employees

Excitement and
enthusiasm are
contagious.

CHAPTER 12

Neutralize Sappers and Hire Zappers

Feeling tired lately? If so, the chances are good you are spending too much time with energy-depleting coworkers.

Corporations are fueled by the combined energy of all employees. This energy can be generated by many sources, such as enthusiastic salespeople, quality-conscious production workers, or caring managers.

Yet, within any company there are individuals who, either because of their natures or attitudes, drain valuable horsepower from the company.

These people, called *sappers*, play politics and constantly bite the hand that feeds them—their company. Sappers wear people down through criticizing, talking too much, causing confrontations, bragging constantly, playing one person against another, and not listening. Sappers drain the life and spirit out of everyone.

Consider sappers as cancerous. They should be removed because they often get their highs out of creating dissension, conflicts, and chaos. Failure is their success.

— ❖ —

A SAPPER'S SUCCESS IS FAILURE.

— ❖ —

MINIMIZE SAPPERS AND FUEL GROWTH, DEVELOPMENT, AND ENTHUSIASM.

— ❖ —

The challenge for executives is to minimize the number of sappers within the organization and look toward recruiting *zappers*, who are the fuel for growth, development, and enthusiasm.

The zapper, unlike the sapper, lifts spirits and infuses life into everyone. When you finish meeting with a zapper, your energy level is increased and gray skies start looking blue.

Zappers make excellent managers, salespeople, and supervisors. However, to be a motivator, such people don't have to don pom-poms and give the *rah! rah! rah!* routine. The primary prerequisite for a zapper is the ability to energize others through personal contact. Zappers are people you look forward to seeing because they build confidence and enhance good feelings.

The acid test for distinguishing zappers from sappers is simply to measure your willingness to spend time with either one. We all have family, friends, and coworkers who add to our pleasures, but we also have uncles, acquaintances, or managers whom we avoid at all costs because of their negative impact on our state of mind.

We all possess the ability to zap or sap, depending on the degree of energy we receive. If we get zapped, we are likely to zap others. Corporations cannot prosper with sappers in high-level positions. Imagine having a sapper in sales or personnel. It would only be a matter of weeks before the employees and customers were sapped themselves.

To identify sappers, executives should look for individuals who:

- *Talk too much.* People who take an hour to say what can be explained in five minutes wear thin and drain energy from people who truly listen.

- *Forecast bad news.* Sappers derive great pleasure in being the first to announce downturns in business, sicknesses, and layoffs that can create disharmony within the company.

---❖---

A ZAPPER'S CREED:

MOTIVATE
ACTIVATE
LIFT SPIRITS
INFUSE LIFE
BUILD CONFIDENCE

---❖---

- *Invite failure.* These pessimists are quick to point out all the risks and reasons why programs will fail, as opposed to talking about how their participation will help a new change succeed.

Sappers do not rise to the occasion through group successes. Sappers are particularly dangerous in small office environments and around impressionable young workers.

If there is a morale problem within your group, or if you feel mentally exhausted at the end of each work day, there is a good chance a sapper exists in the group. Even worse, the sapper could be you.

What we say today might mean something else tomorrow.

CHAPTER 13

Managers Must Act as Filters to Protect Their People

When an oil filter breaks down, allowing dirt to penetrate a car's engine, mechanical failure and problems are inevitable. When managers neglect to filter information disseminating from the top, personnel problems, politics, and miscommunications abound.

Take the example of a company that was contemplating a change in the organizational structure of the salesforce. During a preliminary meeting, top executives from sales, marketing, and customer service suggested a number of changes. Several of the ideas translated into the elimination of two positions in the field.

After the meeting, the customer service manager discussed the possible cutback with his representatives. It was only a matter of minutes before all the salespeople in the field got wind of the rumor. This premature announcement by the manager caused an upheaval. The rumors and conjectures started to roll into a big unstoppable ball. Everyone was on edge, wondering who would be laid off and what would be cut.

77

—— ❖ ——

MANAGERS WHO IGNORE THEIR ROLES AS
INFORMATION FILTERS WILL ENCOUNTER
PERSONNEL PROBLEMS, POLITICS, AND
MISCOMMUNICATIONS.

—— ❖ ——

Irresponsible actions like this one create apprehension for the workers. Managers must be strong enough to avoid leaking confidential information, airing dirty laundry, or announcing personnel changes before the employees are notified. In other words, supervisors must work as filters to stop conjectures and innuendoes that would be disruptive to an employee's positive state of mind.

Once, when I was a director of sales, my boss approached me and requested that I inform the salespeople of the company's decision to curtail paying the difference in cost between a green and gold American Express card. Upon investigation, I discovered that only one individual had a gold card, which translated into twenty-five dollars of extra cost. Since I was working hard to focus this person on selling and building customer relationships, I chose not to broach the card cost at that time.

Making an issue of the credit card, as requested by my manager, would have slowed momentum, changed focus, and resulted in hours of discussions within the sales group about the home office's pettiness. After all, the cost was minimal, and a good salesperson would find a way to bury the added cost in other expenses. It was a matter that didn't deserve top priority at the time.

Always keep in mind that subjects like compensation, staffing, or price, change in scope several times before final implementation. That is why it is best to hold announcements until they are carefully considered and etched in stone.

Another problem that managers confront is the risk of adding their own personal feelings to messages that emanate from the top. Here, also, managers must function as filtering mechanisms, but in this case they must minimize personal biases.

For instance, if a CEO mandates new policies on company cars and orders supervisors to disseminate the information, some managers might slant their presentations because of a poor working relationship with the CEO or a distaste for change. Managers in these cases must avoid comments that exhibit indifference or even hostility. For example, "It's the

— ❖ —

RELEASING INFORMATION BEFORE IT IS FACT
CAN CAUSE A BREAKDOWN IN YOUR
COMPANY'S ENGINE.

— ❖ —

MANAGERS MUST FILTER PERSONAL FEELINGS
FROM INFORMATION THAT EMANATES FROM
THE TOP.

— ❖ —

petty attitude of my boss and the company. I don't think they should stop paying for the maintenance of the cars. It's a joke. I didn't have a thing to do with it."

This unfiltered approach will damage the department and the corporate culture. Supervisors must look beyond minute differences and accommodate the personnel and top executives without slanting information. If there is a problem, it's best to deal with it on a personal level.

In the long run, releasing any information before it is fact or disseminating messages with personal biases can cause a breakdown in your company's engine—your people.

Doing and directing
require two distinctly
different sets of skills.

CHAPTER 14

Beware: The Best Workers Do Not Always Make Good Managers

The best workers don't necessarily make good managers. This statement proves true daily, as supervisors promoted from the ranks fail miserably in making the transition from a worker to a boss.

But, while searching for the cause of the ineffective manager, most executives are quick to point out the shortcomings of the individual rather than take an objective look at the selection and training process.

Most supervisors promoted from within never make it for one of three reasons:

1. *Wrong attitude.* The first reason new supervisors can't cut it is because they lack the appropriate attitude, education, or intellect necessary to make the transition; they have been promoted because of their in-depth technical knowledge. For example, technicians and pure mechanics who are task-oriented performers may not make good supervisors because they have real difficulties in dealing with gray areas and qualitative issues.

—— ❖ ——

MANAGERS HIRED FROM WITHIN NEVER
MAKE IT FOR THREE REASONS:

WRONG ATTITUDE
IMPROPER TRAINING
LACK OF SUPPORT

—— ❖ ——

WORKERS HAVE MANAGERS; MANAGERS
SHOULD HAVE MENTORS.

—— ❖ ——

2. *Improper training.* The second reason many managers fail is poor or inadequate training in communication skills. Managers promoted from within have a tendency to tell employees how to do a job instead of explaining what needs to be accomplished within a specified period. This action fosters frustration, inhibits creativity, and depletes the desire of employees to assume ownership of assigned work.

3. *Lack of support.* The final reason managers fail is lack of accessibility to seasoned top executives who could coach the new manager during the early weeks of the new assignment. All great performers—whether they are musicians, athletes, or managers—can quickly point to a mentor who helped and encouraged them during their growth years.

In selecting a new manager from within, it is important to look beyond the technical aspects of performance and seek out individuals who:

- *Think before they act* and carefully choose their words when communicating with others, whether verbally or in writing. A common problem within management ranks appears to be a severe lack of critical writing and thinking skills.

- *Listen to others' concerns*, including upper-level executives and colleagues. Listening is a sure-fire way to develop an attitude of caring and concern. If the prospective manager can develop this kind of personality, it will be easy for him or her to promote good working relationships with employees.

- *Participate and assume leadership roles* in outside organizations like the PTA or the Boy Scouts. This kind of activity can only add to the well-rounded personality needed by new supervisors.

- *Demonstrate respect* for supervisors and coworkers alike.

— ❖ —

PROSPECTIVE MANAGERS MUST DISPLAY
AN ABILITY TO:

THINK
LISTEN
PARTICIPATE
RESPECT
VALUE
CHALLENGE

— ❖ —

- *Value the principles, practices, and procedures of the company.* Dedication to a mission is impossible without a clear understanding of the company's objectives.

- *Challenge upper-level decisions* when they do not appear to be in the best interest of an individual or the company. The new manager must be capable of weighing important criteria in making key decisions.

Building an effective management team from within requires careful selection, timely training, and patience to provide guidance.

Exposing the right people to an appropriate environment will insure personal and professional success for them in their new roles as managers. New supervisors tossed into a sink-or-swim situation have little chance of surviving shark-infested waters.

Our respect for another person either increases or decreases over time. It never stays the same.

CHAPTER 15

Employee Selection Takes Time and Patience

Most employees discharged for poor performance are not incompetent. They are victims of management's inadequate selection process. People fail because their skills, personal chemistry, and backgrounds do not accurately match with the requirements of their job.

For example, an introverted electrical technician, accustomed to working within a controlled environment, will miss the mark if transferred to a field sales position 1,000 miles from the home office.

Attention needs to be focused on why managers continue making errors in selection that result in frustrated employees and large turnovers. Our research indicates three primary sources that create this problem.

1. *Poor interviewing techniques.* The interview process is the executive's first opportunity to determine whether candidates possess the personality and skills necessary to fill positions.

—— ❖ ——

KEYS TO AN EFFECTIVE SELECTION PROCESS:

GOOD INTERVIEWING TECHNIQUES
FLEXIBLE PERSONNEL POLICIES
ACCURATE JOB DESCRIPTIONS

—— ❖ ——

The interviewer needs to accurately assess accomplishments and determine whether people truly represent their stated qualifications. In other words, the interrogator must avoid being snowed.

The best way to dig below the surface is to ask non-challenging questions that require candidates to cite specific examples that support their positions. For example, "Your philosophy of employment involvement is interesting. Talk to me about some successes you have recently had with this approach toward managing." If prospective employees struggle to provide concrete examples, it is time for more probing.

The interviewer must also avoid tipping-off candidates in the early stages of a meeting by revealing preferences in areas such as employment history, management theories, and personal interests. If prospects are told that technical acumen is important, sharp individuals may pick up on the statement and play on it throughout the meeting. This will result in an inaccurate perception of the candidate.

Furthermore, many managers fail to recognize that shortcomings in character and personal chemistry cannot be overcome with training and exposure. Hiring people in hopes of changing apparent flaws is a tremendous mistake.

And the one activity most interviewers ignore is listening. How many times have you been in interviews where managers have elaborated continually on their accomplishments without listening to your background and successes? Think about the negative feelings you received from those interviews because you knew the person could not make a qualified choice.

2. *Strict personnel policies.* Many companies have policies that eliminate positions not filled at the start of a fiscal year. This policy causes managers to make quick decisions to avoid losing the slots. Unfortunately, in the interest of saving time, employees, who lack both training and skills, are usually selected from within the same department.

3. *Inadequate job descriptions.* Another clear-cut reason for job failure is the absence of understandable job descriptions. If managers really don't recognize what skills are needed

—— ❖ ——

MANAGERS SHOULD BE ENCOURAGED,
NOT PENALIZED, FOR BEING METHODICAL
IN THEIR HIRING PRACTICES.

—— ❖ ——

to successfully perform the requirements of positions, there's no reasonable way to select appropriate candidates.

These three problems often lead to faulty hiring and the wrongful discharge of employees, actions that can have both ethical and financial implications. Employee turnover negatively affects morale, decreases the efficiency of existing workers, and burdens the company in the form of severance pay and unemployment compensation.

For these reasons a good selection process should involve plenty of preparation. Managers should be encouraged, not penalized, for being methodical in their hiring and interviewing practices. Policies should allow flexibility in testing internal candidates before a final commitment is made.

Also, interviewing should be conducted by managers who have a clear understanding of the job requirements so they can arrive at an accurate assessment of candidates' qualifications.

Remember: Getting who and what you want is a process that takes time and patience.

History is the best
indicator of what will
happen in the future.

CHAPTER 16

References—A Critical Quality-Control Check Before Hiring

Checking the references of a potential employee should not be a rubber-stamp procedure. References, even when supplied by the candidate, can reveal important character traits and work habits that failed to surface during the interview process.

It's astounding what a reference check can yield with a proper approach that applies a good line of questioning. In fact, over the years our clients have eliminated ten percent of their best candidates after professional or personal problems surfaced during comprehensive reference checks.

The time to confirm a favorable perception of important new hires is before, not after, they join the company. There is no substitute for a thorough and objective reference check that independently reveals the background and skills of a candidate.

To insure that a reference check will facilitate the hiring of excellent workers, try the following five techniques during the conversation.

1. *Disarm the reference.* To obtain a real picture of a prospective employee, the individual giving the reference has to be disarmed. This can be accomplished by explaining that

— ❖ —

CHECKING REFERENCES SHOULDN'T BE
A RUBBER-STAMP PROCEDURE.

— ❖ —

REFERENCES ALLOW YOU TO CONFIRM
YOUR PERCEPTION OF A NEW HIRE
BEFORE, NOT AFTER, YOU HIRE.

— ❖ —

the check is only a formality. The person giving the reference should be made to feel that any information provided will not disqualify the candidate but be utilized for constructive purposes.

2. *Never show surprise.* Another posture needed to gain an accurate perception is not showing surprise when a sensitive element is disclosed. For example, if the person giving the reference starts discussing a problem the candidate had with a former manager, it is best to maintain a neutral position. This tactic provides a comfortable situation in which the person can open up, because, supposedly, nothing new is being revealed. Shocked responses like "Bob didn't get along with his boss?" or "This guy really seems to be a pot-stirrer!" will negate the remainder of the dialogue.

Questions during this process should be open-ended and nonchallenging. For example, "Tell me about how Bob related to others in his group?" or "If you were hiring Bob, what type of training programs would you suggest for his personal growth and development?" The answers to these questions will provide input for further questions.

3. *Be alert for perfect references.* It should be pointed out that there is no such animal as a perfect candidate. Everybody has strengths and weaknesses that are evident to others. A flawless reference check that does not reveal any weaknesses or conflicts should send up a flare. This type of reference is often the result of a well-coached player who is a close friend or an employer who would be happy to see the candidate leave.

4. *Investigate negative statements.* Negative statements can actually be positive if the candidate created conflict in an attempt to act responsibly. In one instance, a foreman was negatively viewed by his subordinates. He was portrayed as a martinet who was at odds with his people. Upon further investigation, however, it was found that the supervisor was only doing his job in enforcing safety procedures at a high-tech assembly plant. Essentially, the manager was protecting the employees while keeping the plant's safety record flawless.

--- ❖ ---

EVERYBODY HAS STRENGTHS AND
WEAKNESSES. AN IMPECCABLE REFERENCE
CHECK SHOULD SEND UP A FLARE.

--- ❖ ---

5. *Ask for a less-than-favorable reference.* It is also acceptable to ask for a reference that the person feels will not be too positive, for example, a coworker who has competed with the candidate. This kind of reference can provide a picture of the individual under the worst of circumstances. It's easy to find a successful manager who functions well when the team is winning. But that same winner may turn into a loser when faced with adversity. Every angle must be checked meticulously.

In addition, when requesting references from a candidate, it is best to secure the names of former bosses, peers, and—in the case of a management candidate—the names of a few subordinates.

Lastly, it is wise to have an impartial person who interviewed the candidate check the references instead of the manager who needs the employee. A sales manager traveling five days a week because of a shortage of two salespeople will definitely tend to jump at the first candidate who owns a briefcase and knows the way to the airport.

Questions are a wonderful way to show you respect the opinions of others.

CHAPTER 17

Focused Questions Create Accountability

As a manager, have you ever been faced with this kind of conversation?

"Victor, how's the production line running?"

"Great! We're getting 2,500 parts an hour."

"Excellent! Keep up the good work."

"Thanks, boss."

All appears well with the production line. Victor is happy. The boss is pleased with above-average output. What could go wrong?

Enter the quality assurance manager.

"Hey boss, remember you told me about the great job Victor was doing?"

"Yes . . . Why?"

"Every part done on Victor's shift has a visual defect. They're going to have to rework one-hundred percent of the production lot."

"You've got to be kidding!"

—— ❖ ——

THE RIGHT QUESTIONS WILL GET YOU
THE RIGHT ANSWERS.

—— ❖ ——

EFFECTIVE QUESTIONS ARE:

CONCISE
OPEN-ENDED (CAN'T BE ANSWERED
WITH YES OR NO)
NONCHALLENGING

—— ❖ ——

Red-faced and embarrassed, the boss hunts down Victor.

"Hello, boss. The line is really humming tonight."

"Never mind humming, Victor. When I asked you yesterday how the line was running, you told me, great. Today, I found out that all the parts were out of spec. Did I hear you right?"

"You sure did, boss. The line was running great, but you never asked if they were all good parts."

Right answer! Wrong question!

This dialogue demonstrates one of the more common sources of problems for managers: not knowing how or when to ask the right questions.

Questions are a manager's quality-control check on the level of understanding and commitment within a department. To be effective, questions should be concise, open-ended (cannot be answered with a yes or no), and nonchallenging.

The primary objective of questions should be to confirm the employee's understanding of a task. For example, "Victor, would you please explain to me your idea of a good quality part?" Or, to solicit input and feedback, a question could be, "Victor, what steps do you think we can take to insure this quality problem will not occur again?"

A wonderful byproduct of well-intended questions is that accountability is created once the employee is drawn into the decision-making process. Employees want to be shown attention and welcome an opportunity to tell how they can improve performance to help the company make more money.

"Thanks for asking, boss. I have this idea that I think can save the company a whole load of money. This is great! First, we . . ."

The chances are that Victor has a viable idea or two. And his self-esteem as a worker will be lifted to new heights because his boss asked for his opinion. Then, once Victor sees an idea of his utilized, he will do every thing possible to successfully complete the job. Victor will be accountable for his work since he initiated it.

— ❖ —

EMPLOYEE ACCOUNTABILITY IS
ENHANCED ONCE THE WORKER IS PART
OF THE DECISION-MAKING PROCESS.

— ❖ —

Furthermore, a manager who utilizes questions as often as statements can avoid hearing the four most dreaded phrases when a problem surfaces:

"You should have asked!"

"That's not my job!"

"I didn't understand!"

"I knew it wouldn't work!"

Accountability is created by an attitude of caring and concern for the employees and the work they perform. The right questions demonstrate care about the workers not only as human beings but also as contributors to the company's success.

It's very difficult to be a "Hands On" and a "Hands Off" manager at the same time.

CHAPTER 18

Good Bosses Manage and Poor Managers Boss

The difference between a good boss who manages and a poor manager who bosses lies in the word *how*.

Effective managers achieve success by explaining:

What needs to be accomplished. "We've got a new order to assemble six hundred P1349 motors."

When the task needs to be completed. "But, we have to have them completed by next Friday."

Why a specific assignment is important. "If we finish the job on time and within the specs, a lot more business has been promised by the customer."

However, the mistake usually made by managers is then telling subordinates *how* to do the job. "Now, this is how I want the whole operation to work. If you follow my directions, we shouldn't have any snags."

—— ❖ ——

EFFECTIVE MANAGEMENT:

EXPLAINS WHAT NEEDS TO BE DONE
TELLS WHEN IT IS TO BE COMPLETED
GIVES REASONS WHY A JOB IS IMPORTANT

—— ❖ ——

Once a manager crosses the line and becomes heavily involved in the details of how to design a part, engineer a new system, or solve a recurring problem, the employees' motivation to be creative and innovative is lost.

Managers must try to avoid the "nitty-gritty syndrome" that involves looking over shoulders and doing instead of directing. Both actions send distinct signals that elicit definitive employee responses.

Looking over shoulders. By looking over employees' shoulders, a manager implies a lack of confidence in the employees. "Doesn't he trust any of us? I get sick and tired of him looking over my shoulder all the time. It drives me crazy. I'm so nervous. I'm a wreck by the end of the shift. He obviously doesn't have any confidence in us."

Doing instead of directing. When a manager spends most of the time doing rather than directing, managerial insecurities quickly rise to the surface. "Why does she need us on this job? She does every thing herself. Is she trying to justify her position? Doesn't she remember when she was one of us?"

Instructing employees on how to do things also removes a built-in quality-control check of ownership if a project goes off track.

Take the example of a manager who instructs a production worker to perform a motor assembly in a specific sequence. Unexpectedly, rejects in another department create a shortage of one component that could delay the assembly of the motor according to the manager's dictated sequence. The result will be lost production, even if the worker knows efficient ways to bypass the missing part through subassemblies. A manager who puts his mark on a project forfeits the right to hold an employee accountable for performance.

The delicate balance here is to be involved and accessible without becoming too hands-on. Never be afraid to delegate responsibilities to the workers. Not only will it add to employee accountability, but also to self-esteem. The subordinate then becomes a contributor as well as a worker.

—— ❖ ——

AS A MANAGER, BE INVOLVED AND
BE ACCESSIBLE—WITHOUT BEING
TOO HANDS-ON.

—— ❖ ——

INCLUDE EMPLOYEES IN THE DECISION-
MAKING PROCESS TO ENHANCE THEIR
ACCOUNTABILITY.

—— ❖ ——

The following suggestions will be helpful for the managers who most commonly have difficulties letting go—those promoted from the ranks.

- *Be patient* when you can do a job in half the time of new workers. Their way may prove more effective in the long run.

- *Be willing* to let others make the same small mistakes you made during the learning process. There's no better teacher than failure.

- *Solicit ideas and suggestions* before you start a project, not after your carefully dictated approach fails.

- *Remember where you came from.* Reflect on how you felt when former bosses reduced your function to nothing more than a technician by telling you how to get a job done. No one wants to be thought of or treated like a machine all the time.

- *Explain why* a task needs to be undertaken. Listen to challenges and criticisms that may arise. Criticism opens the door to holding employees accountable by doing a job their way.

Following these suggestions will activate your group to out-perform even your highest expectations. This will then lead to the motivation necessary for continued success.

Layoffs are a symptom of
a deep rooted problem in
a company.

CHAPTER 19

Management Controls Can Prevent Layoffs

It is always puzzling when corporate press releases announce forthcoming layoffs as "necessary due to a slowdown in customer orders." Most layoffs occur because *costs are out of control* and not as a result of sales cycles.

When profits begin eroding, most executives react by taking the easiest and the most visible route to cutting costs—layoffs.

And once the layoff dialogue begins between managers, two comments always seem to crop up:

"This layoff will help us get rid of the dead wood."

"We definitely have too many people sitting around with nothing to do."

My first question to these executives is always "who are you going to fire from within this group for letting the head count get out of control?"

— ❖ —

LAYOFFS AREN'T A PANACEA FOR
FINANCIAL WOES.

— ❖ —

A DECREASE IN PROFITS DOESN'T HAVE TO
MEAN A DECREASE IN EMPLOYEES.

— ❖ —

**STEPS TO AVOID THE OVERSTAFFING
DILEMMA:**

MONITOR SALES/EMPLOYEE RATIO
USE AUTHORIZATION/SIGN-OFF FORMS
UTILIZE OVERTIME
HIRE TEMPS
TRY PART-TIMERS

— ❖ —

Most companies, particularly when business is strong, neglect to monitor or audit the addition of new employees. Sure, hiring freezes and other edicts emanate from the top when a blip occurs in the quarterly earnings, but long-term standards, policies, and authorizations (sign-offs) for hiring are nonexistent in many companies.

Executives often forget that an employee earning $30,000 per year constitutes a capital investment in excess of $250,000 over a five-year period. If a company is carrying ten extra people, this translates into $2,500,000 in lost profits.

The sensible way to avoid being over staffed is to institute three sound business practices.

1. *Develop a sales/employee target.* Sales ratios are calculated by dividing total sales by the number of employees. Typical ratios range from $80,000 to $300,000 depending on the additional value of the product or service. The higher the employee-value added, the lower the necessary ratio.

2. *Developing authorizations or sign- offs.* Authorization or sign-off forms for new hires should circulate through the respective departments—personnel and top management. The benefits of sign-offs are many, including matching the needs of one division with an excess in personnel that might exist at another site. When following this procedure, the hiring manager knows that the president will be reviewing the request, and will think twice before sending out the call for additional people.

3. *Offering overtime.* Another plausible cure to the overstaffing dilemma is using overtime. There are always workers trying to make extra money. The only way for most is to pull overtime. However, many managers frown on the word because they think it translates into waste and overcost. In actuality, overtime can save money by limiting the hiring of additional staff.

Other avenues for avoiding the overstaffing dilemma include utilizing temporary help or hiring part-time employees.

By following these suggestions the next time business slows down, it may be possible to weather the storm without layoffs.

CHAPTER 20

Use the Pen as an Ally,
Not an Adversary

PROBLEM ONE

"The pen is mightier than the sword."

It can also be a dangerous weapon in many business situations, where it can wound both the author and the recipient.

I was once asked to comment on a letter of reprimand to a regional sales manager of a major industrial company whose sales were twenty percent below forecast:

Dear Rick:

Your performance through the third quarter is unacceptable and needs to be improved immediately.

Also, it appears that your salespeople are not being properly managed, as evidenced by the drop in actual sales calls versus last year.

If I don't see a significant change in your attitude within the next 30 days, we will be forced to take action.

Sincerely,

Bob Johnson
President

—— ❖ ——

SOME THINGS ARE BETTER SAID
THAN WRITTEN.

—— ❖ ——

TRY THE FACE TO FACE INSTEAD OF
THE PEN TO PAPER.

—— ❖ ——

Upon reading the letter, I asked three questions:

"Do you want to fire Rick?"

"Would you like Rick to show this letter to his wife?"

"If you can rectify the problems, do you want this letter to be around in the files ten years from now?"

The president's response was a definite "no" to each question. The memo was immediately tossed into the shredder.

Letters, speed memos, or any type of written or verbal communication that can be stored or shared with others should never attack personality, integrity, or morals.

As human beings we frequently make impulsive decisions under the heat of daily pressures. Putting these decisions in writing can only lead to embarrassment and hard feelings when all the facts become apparent at a later date.

Talk problems out, face to face. Letters, when necessary, should stick only to the facts, without emotion and bias.

The point: *Some things are better said than written.*

If you feel the need to write a scathing memo, wait twenty-four hours; sleep on it before releasing it. Somehow, problems just don't appear as severe the following day. Or, reach out and pick up the phone instead of the pen and schedule a face-to-face conversation the next day. You will feel a lot better in the morning.

PROBLEM TWO

Another *pen*-ding dilemma facing most managers is the appropriate use of written communication for daily operational procedures.

All too often employees complain about the tremendous number of useless managerial memos they receive every day. Some managers insist that anything said or scheduled must be transferred to paper, copied, filed, and distributed worldwide.

— ❖ —

EMPLOYEES VIEW EXCESSIVE, INEFFECTUAL
MEMOS AS A WASTE OF TIME AND MONEY.

— ❖ —

When this approach is adopted, significant news tends to get buried in a paper avalanche.

For example, the sales manager of a manufacturing company commonly wrote and distributed three to five (and a record of twelve) daily memos. Most of the sixteen people in the department spent the day on the road with clients. Upon returning to the plant, these salespeople were confronted with the usual telephone messages and a mailbox filled with what they called "white death," the dreaded memo.

The employees thought the memos were insulting, because in many cases the information was viewed as mostly useless, assumed, or common-sensical. Furthermore, those little pieces of managerial "white death" represented a waste of time and money.

On many occasions when the manager did need to communicate a matter of consequence, it was overlooked as just another piece of black-and-white memorabilia.

To eliminate this common problem, managers should only use memos as vehicles for defining objectives, confirming projects, or dealing out praise—topics that can really make a difference. In this case, employees will be more inclined to read your memos than to play wastebasket basketball with them.

You can't get what you
want, until you know
what you want.

CHAPTER 21

Keep Expectations Realistic

Consider the following scenarios.

You present a generous offer to a potential job candidate only to be informed that the compensation package was insulting.

After being part of a company for sixteen years, you are informed that your services are no longer needed because they are looking for someone younger and more educated.

You tried raising prices by ten percent, and many of your customers threatened to move their businesses elsewhere.

After being on time for five years, you arrive fifteen minutes late and are asked by the boss, "Is there a personal problem here?"

Four different situations, four different responses, one common thread: Someone's expectations were shattered, and a misunderstanding was born.

—— ❖ ——

WHEN EXPECTATIONS ARE SHATTERED,
MISUNDERSTANDINGS ARE BORN.

—— ❖ ——

A common situation involving expectations and misunderstandings evolves during employee reviews. For instance, a worker who was praised repeatedly was due for an annual performance review. His expectations were for a fantastic, unbelievable, and phenomenal review—along with a significant raise. Also, to reinforce his bargaining position, this employee relayed the positive comments to a minimum of fourteen fellow employees, plus friends and family members while soliciting their input on the size of his upcoming raise.

The consensus: The employee should receive a minimum increase of ten percent. However, after jawboning with his manager for several hours, he secured a seven percent increase. Only four percent was budgeted for the other employees of the company.

The result: A good employee was disappointed, and a supportive manager was angry.

The problem: Both of these people had different expectations of what constituted a good raise.

To avoid the most common business-related misunderstandings associated with expectations, managers must take three important steps.

1. *Shape employee perspectives.* Accomplish this by being aware that workers look to managers for expectations. When it comes to a salary dispute, as in the previous example, it would not be inappropriate to start talking about budgeted salary increases several weeks before the annual reviews. Such information acclimates the employees' thoughts toward a lower percentage without loss of motivation.

2. *Monitor all messages all the time.* Employee expectations are developed over a long period of time through their interpretation and assimilation of managerial actions. Therefore, it is always important to periodically monitor the messages that you are transmitting. It is very easy to fall into a rut that will make employees hold inconsistent or misleading hopes.

Managers must be aware of the long-term signals they are sending to employees. They must exhibit control in releasing important information to insure they are not creating false

— ❖ —

EXPECTATIONS SHOULD MATCH REALITY.

— ❖ —

WHAT MOST PEOPLE REFER TO AS CHANGE
IS NOTHING MORE THAN DISJOINTED
EXPECTATIONS.

— ❖ —

expectations that will lead to conflict and poor employee morale.

3. *Send clear signals to customers.* Just as essential as sending precise expectations to employees is sending clear signals to customers so they will know what to expect. If customers have expectations about a product or service, remember that they acquired their hopes only because they were told what to look forward to.

It is important to try to be genuine with customers. Don't make promise upon promise that can't be kept, or the chances are that the company's stature will be diminished.

What most people refer to as change is nothing more than disjointed expectations. By continually monitoring the messages you send to employees and customers, it is easier to insure that their expectations are closely aligned with reality.

The only thing more powerful than peer pressure is peer recognition for a job well done.

CHAPTER 22

Recognition—The Ultimate Motivator

Recognition of a worker's accomplishments is the single most effective long-term motivational tool available to the manager. Good salaries, high commissions, and excellent benefit packages are only small contributors to an employee's level of job satisfaction.

For example, during a presentation at an annual sales meeting of a high-tech company, I witnessed an interesting phenomenon following the distribution of the bonus checks and performance awards for the previous year.

Everyone talked about the awards and congratulated the winners. Not one of the participants ever raised an issue about the bonus checks.

A couple of weeks after this meeting, I was in the field office of the manager who had won the "Most Improved Territory" award. Do you think she had the bonus check framed and hung on her office wall?

Money is frail. Recognition has much more staying power to activate and motivate employees because it has a positive impact on self-esteem. How often have you heard, "They can

— ❖ —

RECOGNITION INCREASES JOB SATISFACTION
AND SELF-ESTEEM.

— ❖ —

FINANCIAL REWARDS WITHOUT
RECOGNITION ARE
COUNTERPRODUCTIVE.

— ❖ —

take my car, my house, my job, but they can't take away my self-respect or pride."

Adopting the following guidelines to reward deserving workers will increase job satisfaction and self-esteem.

- Financial rewards without recognition are counter-productive and will eventually become expected for the performance of normal work duties. But don't be afraid to periodically praise the employees who conscientiously perform those daily activities.

- If financial awards are offered, they should be accessible to the employee's family and limited in scope and duration.

- Rewarding employees with easy assignments demonstrates disparity that will affect relationships with other subordinates.

- Praise employees not only for good performance inside the company, but also for accomplishments in the community—for example, raising money for charities or coaching youth league sports.

- Recognition from the upper levels of the company's management will create a more powerful, positive effect on the employees.

- Use awards and recognition sparingly. Even the best things in life become commonplace or trivial with overuse. Overdoing recognition can reduce the significance of this valuable management tool. That is why many coaches frown upon awarding trophies to young children. It doesn't give the kids anything special to look forward to.

—— ❖ ——

RECOGNITION EMANATING FROM THE TOP
PROVIDES A LONG-TERM, POSITIVE IMPACT.

—— ❖ ——

One more point: Recognition should not be limited to employees. Customers and suppliers should also be made aware that their efforts are appreciated and needed for mutual growth and development.

For example, an executive of a small but growing printing company wanted to show appreciation for the customers' and suppliers' support. A combination open-house and appreciation event was staged. Business was put aside and top executives, managers, and workers were invited to meet and talk with the buyers and suppliers. The time was constructed in which to ask, "What can we do to keep and develop your valued support?"

The event was successful because the customers and suppliers were impressed to see how important they were and would continue to be as contributors to the overall success of the company.

In the final analysis, employees, customers, and suppliers need to be recognized for the valuable role they play in building a company's culture and stature.

Customers want
suppliers who'll be able to
serve them in the years
ahead.

PART III

Responsive Actions
That Show
Customers You Care
About Their Business

Your current customers present the best opportunity for new business. All you have to do is ask.

CHAPTER 23

Avoid Actions and Words That Can Cost You Millions

PROBLEM ONE: ACTIONS OR INACTIONS

I would like to take this opportunity to apologize to the salesclerk I interrupted at the pharmacy. After all, she was talking to her boyfriend on the phone.

I would also like to send condolences to the auto mechanic who screamed at me because I wanted to know the cost of each part that he replaced.

I should also repent for asking advice in a women's boutique while the salesgirl was eating lunch and studying for her SAT exams.

I guess you could say I border on being rude because I expect responsive, courteous service when spending my hard-earned money. When I don't get good service, I complain. The problem is, I'm in the minority, which gives business the false

— ❖ —

PERSONAL SERVICE SHOULD BE THE RULE
AND NOT THE EXCEPTION.

— ❖ —

THREE WORDS THAT CAN COST ANY
BUSINESS MILLIONS:

"IS THAT IT?"

— ❖ —

sense that everything is fine and that most customers are satisfied.

Our expectations of service have dropped to such a low level that any responsiveness is praised rather than expected. Unfortunately, many merchants have picked up on the public's acceptance of lower standards and have given customers what they have come to accept—indifference and unresponsive service.

At the boutique I was chastised by the manager for not being sensitive to the salesclerk's need to study on the job. It was a condition for employment that was allowed when business was slow. Vowing to never impose on their time again, I have since purchased all my gifts through the catalogue of a competitor.

The boutique lost more than a sale. It has forever given up a customer who could purchase a variety of goods and pass recommendations to additional purchasers.

PROBLEM TWO: WORDS

Another extensive problem in the service area involves business failing to focus on *cross-selling* instead of order-taking. Have you ever noticed the most frequent response from a salesperson once you reach the cash register?

"Is that it?"

These three words undoubtedly cost businesses millions in lost sales each year.

For example, I had an opportunity to visit the same doughnut chain in four cities. After ordering coffee at each location, I struggled with the same dilemma: Should I get a doughnut?

"Is that it, sir?"

"Ah . . . Yes . . . That'll be all."

Four shops, four *Is that it*s. And four less doughnuts for me, four more doughnuts for the company to eat.

Although I appreciated the contribution the salesclerks have made to my battle of the bulge, I began to wonder how much additional revenue could be gained if all 8,000 employees

—— ❖ ——

NEVER LET CUSTOMERS WALK OUT THE
DOOR IF YOU HAVE PRODUCTS THEY NEED.

—— ❖ ——

sold one more doughnut each day. It turns out that one extra doughnut would add over $1,000,000 in annual sales to the chain.

The point: Don't let the customers escape if there are any needs that can be filled with products you have on your shelf. Therefore, it is important to train employees in cross-selling techniques.

Here are some sample cross-selling questions that encourage purchasing:

"Would you like a nice, fresh doughnut with your coffee?"

"I have a lovely tie that would go great with that shirt."

"This lamp doesn't have a lightbulb. Do you need any?"

"We just got in a new word-processing program that would be compatible with your computer. Would you like to see a demonstration?"

"Is there anything else we can help you with?"

Cross-selling demonstrates that you are paying attention to customers because you are interested in doing business. Most customers are not experts and welcome suggestions and advice to justify a purchase.

Your business will certainly benefit if you implement a few basic policies that demonstrate responsiveness.

Limit personal calls during working hours. As much attention as possible has to be afforded to your customers. They are paying for goods and services. By having salespeople on the phones and not on the floor, sales will surely falter.

Eliminate eating in all customer areas. This behavior can only be a source of distraction for both the salesclerk and the customers. It displays not only improper etiquette but also a lax attitude or even an air of arrogance.

Demand that recreational reading be done on break or at home. It's not that you don't want employees to be informed and better educated, but any activities that take away from focusing on customers will be viewed as a lack of responsiveness. Whenever someone enters your place of business, insist that salespeople spend time trying to read the needs of the customers.

Discourage prolonged conversations between employees. Having employees who interact on all levels is a blessing. But when the relationships lead to excessive gabbing, the only loser is your business. Nothing is more irritating than looking for a salesperson and finding one who is too busy talking with a fellow worker. This is the easiest way to alienate customers.

Provide sufficient personnel to cover estimated traffic. The two complaints that raise the most negative feelings from customers are "The lines are too long!" and "I can't find anybody to help me!" As a manager you have to be prepared for times of heavy traffic. This will allow customers to feel comfortable about spending money.

Have employees smile—be friendly. It's amazing how much a smile or a friendly, genuine word can positively affect a customer's disposition for spending. Being upbeat will set the tone for a comfortable atmosphere. Most customers don't ask for much more than a good product and a smile after the sale.

Insist that salespeople ask, "Can I help you with anything else?" Cross-selling is a technique that can be easily employed by workers. It doesn't take a whole lot of time and effort. Basically, employees should keep clear of phrases like "Is that it?" or "All set?"

Following these policies will be noticed not only by you, but also by your accountant.

CHAPTER 24

Monitor High Prices That Open the Door to Competition

The greatest single temptation in business is to set prices for your goods or services based on what the customer will bear instead of on the cost and value of the offerings.

With the exception of well-versed and astute industrial purchasing agents, most businesses and consumers are faced with making buying decisions with little knowledge of the real costs and market conditions for most products. As consumers, we are often forced to negotiate one-time purchases such as cars and major appliances with salespeople who have gained a distinct advantage through experience.

Many of these so-called negotiators have obviously dealt with their products for years. They know the ins and outs and will surely use them to influence purchases.

Also, because of their extensive product knowledge, salespeople maintain the upper hand in any buyer–seller situation. They are privy to reports, seminars, or presentations that the consumer never sees. In short, this may be temporarily healthy for sales but is unfortunate for the consumer.

—— ❖ ——

THE GREATEST SINGLE TEMPTATION IS
TO BASE PRICES ON WHAT THE CUSTOMER
WILL BEAR.

—— ❖ ——

All of this means that there is a tremendous temptation for businesses to generate sinful margins based on the inattention of the buyers.

Take the example of the owner of a high-rise office building who was paying $1,000 a month for what appeared to be a unique maintenance service from a nearby supplier. After noticing that the service only took a few hours, the building owner decided to secure quotes from two out-of-town suppliers. The result: The highest quote was six-hundred dollars less than the current cost, and the local supplier lost the maintenance contract, a friend, and possible referrals.

This exemplifies that it may take a week, a month, or a year, but eventually, through education and word of mouth, customers become aware of the value of their purchases. If customers discover that they have been had with unusually high prices, relationships die, credibility suffers, referrals disappear, and new competition steals the business.

The most interesting facet of price gouging is that it occurs most frequently with current customers, friends, and associates, not strangers or new customers. This is true because human nature dictates you leverage knowledge, emotions, and the needs of friends or current customers simply because it's convenient. Imagine the family problems that would be caused if you moved your insurance coverage from an uncle who owns an agency. The implications for business are even greater.

The next time you think about making changes, whether with new customers or established ones, consider that prices should conform to three standards.

1. *Remain consistent.* Constant fluctuations in prices are a sign of disorganization or even dishonesty. Customers pick up on changes more quickly than you think. Once they catch on, the inconsistencies may then be used as leverage for future purchases or they may simply seek another supplier for the same product.

2. *Reflect costs and market values.* Developing a customer–supplier relationship is based on how much your business can be trusted. If you try to raise prices solely with ridiculous add-ons or excuses, the customers will object and

—— ❖ ——

PRICES SHOULD REFLECT COSTS AND VALUES,
NOT FEELINGS AND RELATIONSHIPS.

—— ❖ ——

DISCRIMINATING PRICES WILL ONLY CREATE
EMBARRASSING CONFRONTATIONS.

—— ❖ ——

maybe lose permanent confidence in your product. Prices should be in line with actual costs that bear out current market values.

3. *Be applied equitably.* Offering different prices to customers based on feelings or relationships can cause confrontations. To remove the temptation of price discrimination, try publishing a price list for your products and services. It may be the quality-control check needed to avoid embarrassing confrontations in the future. You don't want to be involved in a situation where a customer asks, "I heard that company X got the same machine parts for four-hundred dollars less per lot. What's going on here? You told me that was the best you could do. Does this happen a lot?"

Fluctuating prices without viable reasons is like rolling dice. In the short run you may score the big winner, but the longer you play, the more likely you are to lose.

Current customers
talk to potential customers
. . . who talk to other
potential customers . . .

CHAPTER 25

Recognize That Every Sale
Is Important

It is common knowledge that many retailing giants are facing flat sales, significant losses, and—in some instances—bankruptcy. What's shocking about the poor performance is that these companies have reasonable prices, brand-name products, and high-traffic locations.

The problem, then, is that retailers make it too difficult for customers to buy and, if they walk away without buying, no one shows concern.

Long checkout lines, indifferent salespeople (if you can find any), and restrictive return policies are all examples of inconveniences that can make shopping a chore worse than mowing a one-acre lawn on a hot day.

Consider the plight of the family that decided to purchase six-thousand dollars worth of appliances from a highly advertised retail giant. Upon arriving at the store, they spent fifteen minutes to locate a salesperson, who then confessed he knew nothing about appliances. In an effort to be helpful, he suggested the customers wait thirty minutes for the department manager to return from lunch.

❖

MEGA-RETAILERS MUST ADOPT THE SMALL
COMPANY'S ATTITUDE.

❖

Since they had traveled twenty miles to patronize the store, they decided to wait and get the purchase out of the way.

When the manager returned, she was interrupted seven times for phone calls during the order-taking process. As the order was being written up—two hours after the family had entered the store—the customers were advised that there would be a fifty dollar delivery charge, a seventy-five dollar set-up cost and an additional eighty dollars to take out all the old appliances.

Furthermore, the department manager suggested that the customers purchase extended warranties, since the store did not coordinate service for the different manufacturers.

Crushed and upset, the customers sought out the general manager to seek relief from all the nickel and dime add-ons. "I'm sorry, those charges are dictated by corporate policy," was the decision-maker's response to the customers, who were ready to plunk down six-thousand dollars.

"Well, if there isn't anything you can do, then we'll just have to take our business elsewhere!"

After a slight pause and a sigh, the manager replied, "I wish I could help, but if you want to go somewhere else, that's up to you."

Rightfully insulted by the overall treatment, the customers left without making the purchase. Later that day they picked up the same appliances from a local shop at a slightly higher price. However, there weren't any additional charges, and all service was coordinated "in store." Within the next thirty days, these satisfied customers recommended the smaller appliance store to friends, who also purchased all their products for a new home.

The major difference between the retail giant and the small shop lies in the attitude of the top executives. Not making a sale or satisfying the customers had no direct impact on the manager of the retail giant. His paycheck did not reflect the lost sale, and it is doubtful if he even cared about the incident.

The small entrepreneur was grateful for the business because the sale would immediately affect the bottom line. Every step was taken to satisfy the customer.

——— ❖ ———

SALESPEOPLE HAVE TO BE TRAINED ABOUT
THE TECHNICAL PRODUCTS THEY SELL.

——— ❖ ———

MAKING PURCHASES EASY AND FUN WINS
REPEAT BUSINESS.

——— ❖ ———

If mega-retailers are to compete in the future, they need to exhibit the small company's attitude that each sale is important. This can be accomplished by structuring compensation programs to reinforce that philosophy. These companies must also allocate money to educate personnel on the technical aspects of products. Retailers that cannot provide value added through service, product knowledge, and convenience will not survive.

On the other hand, small specialty shops and catalog houses have exemplified the fact that making the buying process easy and fun is the simple way to win repeat business and referrals from educated buyers.

Keep in mind that the approaching decades will be marked by demanding customers who will be out to make discriminating purchases. Location, prices, and brand names alone will not guarantee success. Embracing customers with a sincere attitude will win out over fancy slogans and buttons whose claims are not supported by actions.

Complaints are an off-handed way for customers to show you they really need you.

CHAPTER 26

Treat Customer Complaints as Opportunities to Gain New Business

Do any of the following complaints sound familiar?

"Your prices are too high!"

"Your quality stinks!"

"I've gotten better service at a self-service gas station!"

"Isn't there any way we can work this out?"

Complaints and objections like these are the clearest indication that customers need and want to continue doing business with your company.

Customers who have viable alternatives to your goods and services will avoid complaining and go elsewhere with their business. Ignoring complaints is like disregarding strange noises in your car's engine: It's a mistake that will cost you later.

——— ❖ ———

COMPLAINTS: AN OPPORTUNITY TO BUILD SOLID CUSTOMER RELATIONSHIPS.

——— ❖ ———

For this reason, complaints and objections should be welcomed as an opportunity to build solid customer relationships. Often the connections between companies and customers are based solely on money matters. However, relationships built on concern for mutual growth and development are the ones that insure success on both ends. It is also a good idea to utilize complaints as a way to demonstrate commitment to building a genuinely service-minded business.

Besides building relationships, problems make it possible to meet with key decision-makers. Meetings with essential executives can positively affect your business. Industrial salespeople are always faced with the struggle and frustration of trying to get by the purchasing department to meet other influential decision-makers within an organization. Problems like incorrect packaging, missed shipments, and product defects are a natural entry into the back offices to begin new relationships with quality managers, plant superintendents, and shipping clerks.

Also, it is imperative to remember that complaints and objections are directly related to service. Even if the product is defective, responsive service can rectify the problem. Since this is the case, keep in mind that service is measured by three standards.

1. *Dealing efficiently with problems.* The ability of your operation to resolve problems quickly, with minimal hassle, speaks well for your company's stature. Being responsive demonstrates reliability and dependability, key words in the service area. A company that responds slowly foregoes chances to develop true customer relationships.

2. *Satisfying customers.* Satisfied customers know that problems will be alleviated at the source. To judge how successfully customers' needs are being addressed, just ask. Be prepared to get an earful. Next, it is critical to act upon the responses and fully placate customers. They know what you are capable of doing, and that is what they will expect.

3. *Offering support.* In many situations a company can satisfy customers even though a problem cannot be solved immediately. For example, a shipment of critical parts gets lost

❖

SERVICE THE CUSTOMER BY
ASKING FOR SUGGESTIONS, LISTENING,
AND FOLLOWING THROUGH.

❖

SERVICE CUSTOMERS OR THEY WON'T
SERVICE YOU.

❖

in transit, the customer's production line goes down, and it will take a minimum of twenty-four hours to replace the lost parts. You cannot solve the problem of the line being down, but at least you can demonstrate to the customer that you care. This can be accomplished by listening to the frustrations of the customer and, more importantly, by offering your support in finding solutions. There's also nothing wrong with showing that you are upset about a customer's problem. This action will satisfy the consumer, build a strong relationship, and differentiate your company from the competition.

It must also be noted that providing customer service and satisfaction doesn't mean you have to solve every single problem. But by demonstrating that the customers' business is important and that their problems are your problems, you can give your buyers a positive perception of you and your company. Essentially, you must service consumers or they won't service you.

Complaints should be viewed as positive input that provides opportunities to strengthen relationships with customers and solicit new business. Remember that your customers are human and understand that perfection is only possible some of the time.

A customer pays for
the right to be treated like
a customer.

CHAPTER 27

Problem Customers: Listen Before You Leap

Does this dialogue ring a familiar bell?

"Don, I can't believe that shipment of envelopes you *promised* was a day late! What's the problem with you? You held up my entire project. I had fifteen people sitting around with nothing to do for about two hours. Do you treat all your customers like this?"

After hanging up the phone, Don contemplates the conversation. "Doesn't this customer realize that I consistently ship quality products at prices that are only slightly above break-even? He probably has no comprehension of the problems caused each time he changes a delivery date or increases the order size. What's more, if it were not for me being his watchdog, his inventories would be totally out of control."

After a tiny moment of composure, he starts again. "On top of all that, he expects me to be his banker by stringing out payments for ninety days. Imagine the audacity to be upset because I delivered one day late. What an ungrateful customer!"

— ❖ —

EMPLOYEE ACTIONS MIRROR THE ATTITUDES
OF THE MANAGER.

— ❖ —

IT IS NOT WHAT YOU SAY BUT HOW YOU SAY
IT THAT LEAVES AN IMPRESSION.

— ❖ —

Managers often impulsively internalize a situation in this way and unknowingly create a companywide atmosphere of resentment toward the customer. Who is right or wrong isn't important because these situations happen all the time. The unfortunate part of this scenario is that our soldiers sense the frustration and carry the torch long after the initial problem has been resolved.

The result? Strained customer relations.

To avoid falling into this trap, realize that employees and customers alike are more sensitive to *how we talk* than *what we say*.

For example, your sales representative will soon forget the reason you were upset with a customer, but will long internalize your negative feelings. This will lead to a tremendous amount of job stress. First, your sales representative will hold a less-than-favorable impression of the customer. Then the stress and fear will be compounded because your employee must also try to sell to the client.

Second, the build-up of negative energy and stress can only lead to more malicious feelings. But instead of simply displacing the stress onto the one customer, the sales representative will inadvertently spread it like a plague to other customers and employees. Admittedly, a hostile environment doesn't happen overnight, but it's amazing how quickly stress and negative energy can blanket a company and smother its creativity.

The last thing you need is for one or more of your employees to lose customers and then feel good about it. Try to remember that your workers are watching you and will both knowingly and unknowingly reveal your attitudes to the customers. Attitudes reflect strong emotions and form a lasting impression that can lead to conflict.

By learning to listen and then training your employees to listen, most problems and conflicts can be resolved through customer input. It is important to remember that the customer is a person whose actions, just like yours, can be the result of momentary pressures.

—— ❖ ——

WHEN A PROBLEM ARISES, LISTEN BEFORE
YOU LEAP.

—— ❖ ——

By listening you may discover that the angry customer was just called on the carpet by the president; or that a key employee left the department, adding to the workload; or that the customer was suffering a personal problem; or that a battle with weight or cigarettes was being fought.

Whatever the case, your overall performance may not be the problem. It may be hard to think along positive lines, but the key is to listen for obvious cues. Once the customer realizes that you are genuinely listening to the gripe, there may be a release. "Don, listen. I'm really not all worked up with you. It's just that the front office has been all over my back the last few weeks. Plus, we had to lay off three more people. I'm just really strung out."

The big picture: The next time a problem arises take the time to *listen before you leap.*

Who knows, if you're lucky, you may learn that the ungrateful customer has friends he can introduce to you.

Quality minded employees produce good products that satisfy important customers.

CHAPTER 28

Tie Employees to the Product and Customers

One summer I worked for a roofing contractor who had a unique policy concerning performance guarantees. As he clearly stated to us young lads, "We offer an out-of-sight guarantee. Once we are out of sight, there is no guarantee."

This policy, callous as it sounds, provided us young workers with an incentive to do the best possible job to avoid taking advantage of older customers on fixed incomes. In addition to the altruistic objective of doing the job right the first time, we had the added incentive of protecting our personal reputations, because the work was performed within our own communities.

Not one of us wanted to be confronted by a neighbor or friend about the poor job we had done. Basically, we wanted to hear that we were professionals performing great work.

We all took pride in our work and felt that quality problems would reflect a lack of caring and concern. It became a kind of competition. This attitude resulted in no rejects that summer, along with an increase in business for the company owner.

— ❖ —

EMPLOYEES WHO FEEL THAT THEIR
PERSONAL INTEGRITY IS ON THE LINE WILL
WORK HARD TO KEEP IT INTACT.

— ❖ —

The lesson to be learned here is that when employees feel that their personal integrity is on the line, quality improves, good service proliferates, and guarantees are almost never tested because they have become a matter of personal satisfaction.

This is why managers should make every effort to emotionally tie employees to their products and services. Workers will take extra care when performing tasks that secure their integrity.

This self-imposed accountability can be accomplished by educating employees on the application of each product. Too often workers' tasks are so minute that they rarely are able to visualize where their work fits into the big picture. This can cause a lack of motivation stemming from an absence of finality. However, if workers are educated to see how each task fits into the overall scheme, a sense of accomplishment will follow and this will add to job satisfaction.

Next, to further increase employee accountability, allow them to have personal exposure and contact with customers. If employees can share ideas and conversations with customers, a relationship can be built that will inspire quality work and product loyalty. If you were servicing a relative or a complete stranger, who would receive the best treatment? It only makes sense that expanding relationships between customers and workers will enhance pride and accountability on both ends.

This two-pronged approach worked very effectively for one of our clients that produces metal stamping for automobile frames. Quality problems were quickly resolved when our client's machine operator visited the customer's assembly line and witnessed first-hand the impact a small flaw had on the customer's process. Not only did the problems dissolve, but a bond grew between the machine operator and the customer that still provides a barrier for new competitors. Because of this bond, the customer and the workers became committed to successfully completing any project.

When employees understand the application of their products and the process used to convert these goods at the

—— ❖ ——

EMPLOYEES WHO UNDERSTAND THE
APPLICATION OF THEIR PRODUCTS TAKE
OWNERSHIP OF THEIR PERFORMANCE.

—— ❖ ——

CUSTOMER EDUCATION AND CONTACT
CREATE A BUILT-IN WARRANTY.

—— ❖ ——

customer's plant, employees take on ownership and feel responsible for both the quality and performance of the products.

Education and personal contact can provide a built-in warranty program, because product failures will affect not only a customer but also a real person whom your employees know.

To go back to the roofing, there was a funny thing about that "out-of-sight guarantee": it appears that, in over thirty years of business, the owner of the roofing company was never called on the guarantee. Were we duped?

Before a sales person
can sell a product or
service he must first sell
himself.

CHAPTER 29

Employ Likable Salespeople Who Provide Value to Your Customers

The most frequently asked question during my talks to trade and business groups is "What attributes make up the best sales representatives?"

Contrary to popular theories, product knowledge and technical expertise alone will not insure success. Good salespeople who can stand the test of time through repeated customer contact all exhibit some of the following traits.

High energy and enthusiasm. Selling is a grueling profession that requires long hours, travel, and constant exposure to new environments. To survive and infect customers with excitement, salespeople must be energetic and enthusiastic about their products. Lethargic salespeople can send mixed signals about confidence in the product and the urgency of the purchase. In addition, sales representatives must exude excitement about the company and the value of the product to customers. If this level of enthusiasm can't be maintained, prospective buyers will, in turn, show distaste or indifference toward the company and the product. Essentially, good sales professionals

—— ❖ ——

SALESPEOPLE WHO DON'T LISTEN CREATE
APPREHENSION IN THE CUSTOMER'S MIND.

—— ❖ ——

OVERSELLING REDUCES THE VALUE
OF A PRODUCT OR SERVICE.

—— ❖ ——

are not afraid of hard work. They are credible and honest while possessing a distinct desire to satisfy customers.

Good listening skills. To maintain prices, cross-sell, and network for leads, salespeople must be good listeners. One universal complaint about the sales profession is that there is too much talking and not enough listening. A participatory attitude can be demonstrated by good listeners.

Problems often arise because many salespeople don't know how to listen and don't recognize the point at which customers have decided to buy. They continue their hard-sell and inadvertently or consciously make inaccurate performance or service claims.

Overselling ultimately affects the level of respect that customers hold for salespeople. This lack of respect may hinder the successful implementation of price increases without a loss of business. Sharp sales representatives must be able to recognize their value to customers, because this understanding determines how much of a push or a shove will break a relationship. When it's all said and done, good salespeople can differentiate sales situations that call for *selling* from the ones that only require *order taking.*

Ability to turn problems into opportunities. The by-products of close relationships are conflicts, whether they are related to products, quality, deliveries, or pricing. Street-savvy salespeople welcome conflicts as opportunities to demonstrate their performance under pressure. Problems also supply wonderful avenues for meeting key decision-makers, who would normally be difficult to contact without stepping on the toes of purchasing groups.

Effective salespeople treat problems as opportunities, resolve conflict without confrontation, and rise above the fray under difficult circumstances. Individuals who cannot effectively handle the daily problems associated with sales soon fall to the wayside.

The final important characteristic necessary for success in sales is what I refer to as *likability.* All other things being equal, the customers will do more business when the purchasing process is easy and fun. Good salespeople are akin to those

— ❖ —

CUSTOMERS ARE INCLINED TO DO BUSINESS
WITH SALESPEOPLE WHO MAKE PURCHASING
EASY AND FUN.

— ❖ —

great teachers who are stern but fair, witty, and respectable. Projecting this kind of personality is very important because in industrial sales, buyers are always directed to curtail unnecessary contact with suppliers. Therefore, salespeople who can get in the door will keep relationships and sales prosperous.

Product knowledge and technical skills are easier to teach than the characteristics of likability, street smarts, and the work ethic. Look for these traits first, because without a strong foundation the building blocks, industry knowledge and technical expertise, will not be effectively utilized to your company's advantage.

The phone only rings
once for successful
companies.

CHAPTER 30

Automated Answering Systems Require Personal Attention

INVALID ENTRY!!! Please try again.

If not properly designed and managed, automated telephone answering systems can cost you business.

Conveniences like automatic bank tellers, drive-up windows for fast-food chains, and computerized phone-answering systems are examples of technology designed to improve efficiency and facilitate the daily functions of a business.

Regrettably, most of this new technology minimizes interpersonal contact between customers and suppliers. This communication gap can be a source of problems.

For example, while trying to order office supplies, my assistant was once held hostage by a computerized answering system that insisted she spell out the last name of her customer service representative. After struggling with the spelling of Wowoszynck, she felt victory was at hand—until she was transferred to four different voice boxes within the system. She never reached her representative or talked to another human

——— ❖ ———

THE KEY TO AUTOMATION IS SIMPLIFICATION.

——— ❖ ———

being throughout this contrived, mechanical, and technical machination.

As a result of this trying experience, we explored alternative sources and found another supplier with lower prices, free delivery, and a human who answers the phone. We now have a new supplier, and our former supplier with the high-tech telecommunications system lost a customer. Ironically, they don't even know they forfeited the business because none of their voice boxes handle customer complaints.

To be sure, for businesses and agencies that deal with thousands of customers, the concept of using a computerized answering system for routine calls has merit. Ticket agencies, credit card companies, and insurance firms can all benefit from this kind of system. It provides faster access to appropriate departments within a large company or government agency. Likewise, automated answering machines can improve accessibility to individuals who are traveling or can provide a way to reach someone after the main switchboard has closed.

The problem, then, is not with the system itself but with how the system is used and managed. If your business warrants a computerized answering system, there are a few areas to consider when designing and monitoring the system.

Keep recorded instructions short and simple. The shorter the message, the greater the likelihood of understanding. Most people don't like listening to prerecorded messages. They become frustrated when they can't comprehend the instructions. Use a voice that is clear and professional. There are even services that customize such messages.

Monitor hang-ups. Many systems can tell you the number of calls that terminate before completion. Too many hang-ups are a sure sign that the system is not working. Research the probable causes and then make the appropriate modifications.

Prepare, prepare, prepare. If your system requires dialing the extension of an individual, make sure customers have access to these exchanges. Try using the system yourself. Test it with employees. Then incorporate their insights and opinions into a solid system design.

—— ❖ ——

HUMAN ACCESS IS A MUST WITH AUTOMATED
TELEPHONE SYSTEMS.

—— ❖ ——

PEOPLE TALKING TO PEOPLE MAKES GOOD
BUSINESS SENSE.

—— ❖ ——

Provide access to a human being. Design the system so that callers can exit the loop and talk to a person without having to hang up for redialing. Also, make exiting the voice box simple, while making human contact quick.

Tune in to abuses. Keep your ears to the ground for people who are using the system to dodge other employees or suppliers. It can be convenient for someone in sales to activate the answering system just to avoid a particular problem customer.

People talking to people makes good business sense. As technology advances, make sure you keep the lines of communication wide open and, when possible, keep them human.

Managers must
learn to do more with
less by utilizing basic
management approaches
that work.

Putting It Together: Management That Works— The Future

The major challenge facing managers in future years will be to develop proud and responsive employees under difficult economic circumstances.

Companies will continue to downsize and operate with lean staffs in hopes of competing effectively in oversupplied world markets. Therefore, the generalist with skills that cover many areas of a business will rule; the specialist will be confined to research and development roles.

Customers will become fewer and bigger while wielding significant purchasing power. Suppliers that stay close, remain responsive, and grow as partners with their customers will survive and profit.

Quality and service will no longer be major selling features. They will be expected, and employees will take great pride in insuring quality and service never become issues in their quest to capture more of a client's business.

The bottom line: Common-sense business approaches that build pride, shape positive expectations, and emphasize the importance of staying close to the customer will insure success in any market or industry.

As a manager it's your responsibility to set the stage by treating suppliers, employees, and customers with the respect and dignity they deserve as your company's most valued resources.

In the end you'll find it's a simple and straightforward management philosophy that really works.